TRADITIONAL SONGS

I Know an Old Lady

Edited by Ann Owen
Illustrated by Sandra D'Antonio

Music Consultant: Peter Mercer-Taylor, Ph.D.
Associate Professor of Musicology
University of Minnesota
Minneapolis, Minnesota

Reading Consultant: Susan Kesselring, M.A.
Literacy Educator
Rosemount-Apple Valley-Eagan
(Minnesota) School District

PICTURE WINDOW BOOKS
MINNEAPOLIS, MINNESOTA

Traditional Songs series editor: Peggy Henrikson
Page production: The Design Lab
Musical arrangement: Elizabeth Temple
The illustrations in this book were rendered in pen with digital coloring.

PICTURE WINDOW BOOKS
5115 Excelsior Boulevard
Suite 232
Minneapolis, MN 55416
1-877-845-8392
www.picturewindowbooks.com

Printed in the United States of America.
1 2 3 4 5 6 08 07 06 05 04 03

Library of Congress Cataloging-in-Publication Data
I know an old lady / edited by Ann Owen ; illustrated by Sandra D'Antonio.
p. cm. — (Traditional songs)
Summary: Presents an illustrated version of the traditional song along with some
discussion of its folk origins.
Includes bibliographical references (p.   ).
ISBN 1-4048-0150-2 (library binding)
1. Folk songs, English—United States—History and criticism—Juvenile literature.
2. Children's songs, English—United States—History and criticism—Juvenile literature.
3. Children's songs—Texts. [1. Flies—Songs and music. 2. Songs.]
I. Owen, Ann, 1953– II. D'Antonio, Sandra, 1956– ill. III. Series.
ML3551 .I5 2003
[E]—dc21
2002155280

What do you see when you sing a song? Does the music come in colors?

What do you do when you sing a song? Does the melody make you dance?

What do you hear when you sing a song? Do the words tell a story?

Let's explore the sights and sounds of one of our favorite songs.

Do you know the old lady who swallows strange things?

I know an old lady
who swallowed a fly.
I don't know why
she swallowed a fly.

Perhaps she'll die.

5

I know an old lady
who swallowed a spider
that wriggled and wriggled
and tickled inside her.

She swallowed the spider to catch the fly,
but I don't know why she swallowed the fly.
Perhaps she'll die.

I know an old lady who swallowed a bird.
How absurd, to swallow a bird.
She swallowed the bird to catch the spider
that wriggled and wriggled
and tickled inside her.

She swallowed the spider to catch the fly,
but I don't know why she swallowed the fly.
Perhaps she'll die.

I know an old lady who swallowed a cat.
Now fancy that, to swallow a cat!
She swallowed the cat to catch the bird,
  she swallowed the bird to catch the spider
    that wriggled and wriggled
      and tickled inside her.

She swallowed the spider to catch the fly,
but I don't know why she swallowed the fly.
Perhaps she'll die.

I know an old lady who
swallowed a dog.
Oh, what a hog to swallow a dog!
She swallowed the dog to catch the cat,
she swallowed the cat to catch the bird,
she swallowed the bird to catch the spider
that wriggled and wriggled
and tickled inside her.

She swallowed the spider
to catch the fly,
but I don't know why
she swallowed the fly.
Perhaps she'll die.

I know an old lady
who swallowed a cow.
I don't know how
she swallowed a cow.
She swallowed the cow
to catch the dog,

she swallowed the bird
to catch the spider
that wriggled and wriggled
and tickled inside her.

16

I Know an Old Lady

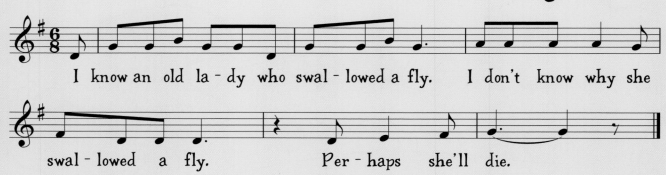

I know an old la-dy who swal-lowed a fly. I don't know why she

swal-lowed a fly. Per-haps she'll die.

2. I know an old lady who swallowed a spider
That wriggled and wriggled and tickled inside her.
She swallowed the spider to catch the fly,
But I don't know why she swallowed the fly.
Perhaps she'll die.

3. I know an old lady who swallowed a bird.
How absurd, to swallow a bird.
She swallowed the bird to catch the spider
That wriggled and wriggled and tickled inside her.
She swallowed the spider to catch the fly,
But I don't know why she swallowed the fly.
Perhaps she'll die.

4. I know an old lady who swallowed a cat.
Now fancy that, to swallow a cat!
She swallowed the cat to catch the bird,
She swallowed the bird to catch the spider
That wriggled and wriggled and tickled inside her.
She swallowed the spider to catch the fly,
But I don't know why she swallowed the fly.
Perhaps she'll die.

5. I know an old lady who swallowed a dog.
Oh, what a hog to swallow a dog!
She swallowed the dog to catch the cat,
She swallowed the cat to catch the bird,
She swallowed the bird to catch the spider
That wriggled and wriggled and tickled inside her.
She swallowed the spider to catch the fly,
But I don't know why she swallowed the fly.
Perhaps she'll die.

6. I know an old lady who swallowed a cow.
I don't know how she swallowed a cow.
She swallowed the cow to catch the dog,
She swallowed the dog to catch the cat,
She swallowed the cat to catch the bird,
She swallowed the bird to catch the spider
That wriggled and wriggled and tickled inside her.
She swallowed the spider to catch the fly,
But I don't know why she swallowed the fly.
Perhaps she'll die.

7. I know an old lady who swallowed a horse.
(Spoken) She died, of course!

About the Song

"I Know an Old Lady" is a favorite of many people. It first showed up in songbooks in the early 1940s. Like many older folk tunes, no one knows who wrote it. It is a kind of traditional song called the cumulative, or repeat, song. In a repeat song, the same tune is repeated as the lines and verses to the song build.

There are many other kinds of folk songs. Some of them are play-party songs (sometimes called singing games), work songs, bragging songs, and nonsense songs.

DID YOU KNOW?

Snakes are animals that really do swallow things whole. They do this because their pointed teeth cannot crush or chew. A snake can open its mouth very wide. This allows the snake to swallow animals larger than itself. Also, its ribs are not connected to each other. They can open wide to let the food move along inside the snake.

23

Make a Wriggling, Tickling Spider

A spider is not like other bugs. It has eight wriggling legs instead of six. You can make an eight-legged spider with pipe cleaners.

WHAT YOU NEED:

- at least 7 black pipe cleaners
- heavy scissors or metal cutters to cut pipe cleaners
- 1 piece of black thread about 1 foot (30 centimeters) long
- an adult to help you

WHAT TO DO:

1. Make two ovals with two pipe cleaners for the two parts of the spider's body.
2. Connect the two ovals by wrapping a small piece of pipe cleaner around them at one end.
3. Cut four pipe cleaners in half for the eight legs. Connect the legs to one oval of the spider's body by wrapping the ends of each piece of pipe cleaner around the sides of the oval. Each side of the oval should have four legs, making eight legs in all. Bend the front two legs forward and the back two legs backward.
4. Cut two small pieces of pipe cleaner and attach them at the front of the spider's head. The spider uses these to feel things.
5. Tie one end of the thread to the middle of the spider. Hang it up and watch it wriggle and tickle—but don't swallow it!

To Learn More

AT THE LIBRARY

Jackson, Alison. *I Know an Old Lady Who Swallowed a Pie.* New York: Dutton Children's Books, 1997.

Krull, Kathleen. *Gonna Sing My Head Off!: American Folksongs for Children.* New York: A.A. Knopf, 1992.

Rounds, Glen, Illustrator. *I Know an Old Lady Who Swallowed a Fly.* New York: Holiday House, 1990.

Sloat, Teri. *There Was an Old Lady Who Swallowed a Trout.* New York: H. Holt, 1998.

Taback, Simms. *There Was an Old Lady Who Swallowed a Fly.* New York: Viking, 1997.

ON THE WEB

CHILDREN'S MUSIC WEB
http://www.childrensmusic.org
For resources and links on children's music for kids, parents, educators, and musicians

NATIONAL INSTITUTE OF ENVIRONMENTAL HEALTH SCIENCES KIDS' PAGES: CHILDREN'S SING-ALONG SONGS
http://www.niehs.nih.gov/kids/musicchild.htm
For music and lyrics to many favorite, traditional children's songs

FACT HOUND
Want more information about traditional songs? FACT HOUND offers a safe, fun way to find Web sites. All of the sites on Fact Hound have been researched by our staff. Simply follow these steps:

1. Visit *http://www.facthound.com.*
2. Enter a search word or 1404801502.
3. Click Fetch It.

Your trusty Fact Hound will fetch the best sites for you!